# NIC GARDNER

# Merchant Navy Survival Guide

*Survive & thrive on your first ship*

# Contents

# I

# Merchant Navy Overview

# 1

# What is the Merchant Navy?

The Merchant Navy or Merchant Marine is a collective term for commercial ships, and includes everything from tankers and cargo ships to ferries and research ships. It isn't the same as the Navy, which is a branch of a country's armed forces. Merchant ships are run by private companies, and are not part of the military.

*Assorted Merchant Ships*

The title "Merchant Navy" was allegedly coined by King George V after World War I, then adopted by other countries. Regardless of where the name came from, careers in the Merchant Navy appeal to people who want something a bit different.

If you've got a sense of adventure, a healthy dose of common sense, and you can deal with the unique challenges of spending half your working life on a ship, it might appeal to you too.

## Merchant Navy vs Navy

If you're thinking of going to sea, it's common to ask, "What's the difference between the merchant navy and the navy?" Well, apart from the fact that one is military and the other isn't, there are several relevant differences:

- most people on most merchant ships have their own cabins;
- depending on your country, the merchant navy usually pays better and has more leave than the navy;
- promotion in the merchant navy is faster;
- merchant crews are usually smaller than naval crews, so you get a broader base of practical experience;
- cargo operations are a large part of operations on merchant ships, while most navy ships don't carry significant quantities of cargo. There are exceptions;
- maritime and commercial law is a large part of officers' and engineers' studies. Naval vessels are often excluded from the requirements of international agreements, and they don't have to deal with commercial law; and
- merchant ships are usually more relaxed and informal than naval ships.

2

# Maritime Law

The International Maritime Organisation (IMO) is the branch of the United Nations (UN) that deals with maritime affairs. According to their website, they're responsible for "…the safety and security of shipping and the prevention of marine and atmospheric pollution by ships."

## Codes & Conventions

The IMO member states agree on Conventions, which are international written agreements on which rules everyone should follow. At a very basic level (you'll go into this in great detail at college), the members agree on the rules, sign the Convention, then go back and make laws in their own countries to implement the rules they agreed on. The IMO has no enforcement power: that's up to the member states.

Codes are recommendations and guidelines for how to implement some part of a Convention. Sometimes they're part of a Convention, sometimes they're separate. Even if they're not technically part of the Convention, it's a good idea to follow them.

There are a lot of Conventions and Protocols (amendments to conventions). At this stage, there are only a few Conventions that you need to know about: they're known as the Four Pillars of Maritime Law.

## 1. International Convention for the Safety of Life at Sea (SOLAS)

SOLAS has rules about how to keep ships and people safe at sea, by building ships properly, carrying proper equipment to communicate and deal with emergencies, and lots more.

## 2. International Convention for the Prevention of Pollution from Ships (MARPOL)

The rules in MARPOL dictate what ships are allowed to throw overboard, where and when it's allowed, and what to do if there's an accident and they spill something. In short, don't throw anything overboard.

## 3. Standards of Training and Certification for Watchkeepers (STCW)

The name is a giveaway: it covers the minimum standards of training for people who work on ships.

## 4. Maritime Labor Convention (MLC)

The MLC is known informally as "The Seafarers' Bill of Rights." It has five sections:

1. minimum requirements for seafarers to work on a ship - age, and medical and training certificates;
2. conditions of employment – wages, working hours, rest and leave; career development;
3. seafarers' accommodation, leisure facilities, and on board catering standards;
4. health and safety, medical care, access to on-shore welfare facilities; and
5. complaints, inspections, responsibilities of the flag and port states.

And two important Codes:

## 1. International Safety Management System (ISM)

This is a result of the sinking of the Herald of Free Enterprise in 1987. According to the IMO, "The objectives of the ISM Code are to ensure safety at sea, prevention of human injury or loss of life, and avoidance of damage to the environment, in particular, to the marine environment, and to property."

## 2. International Ship and Port Security Code (ISPS)

This is a result of the 9/11 attacks. The International Maritime Organization (IMO) says, "The International Ship and Port Facility Security Code (ISPS Code) is a comprehensive set of measures to enhance the security of ships and port facilities, developed in response to the perceived threats to ships and port facilities in the wake of the 9/11 attacks in the United States"

Other Conventions cover everything from collision regulations to ship recycling. You can find a list of Conventions on the IMO website[1].

# 3

# People, Ships & Cargoes

Seafarers are a mixed bunch. I've met people who went to sea in their teens, following in the family trade; people who went to sea in their forties and fifties after a full careers in an office; and everything in-between.

According to the International Chamber of Shipping (ICS), most seafarers come from China, the Philippines, Indonesia, the Russian Federation and Ukraine. Most ratings come from the Philippines, and most officers from China. Despite that, seafarers can and do come from all over the world and all sorts of backgrounds. If you go to sea, be prepared to live and work with people from a wide range of nationalities, religions, beliefs and cultures.

Many engineers and deck ratings started out in a trade, then came to sea. People who have trained in mechanical trades (mechanic, fitter, machinist, and similar) can often have their trade qualifications recognised towards an engineering certificate; electricians and electrical engineers can often get credit towards an electro-technical officer (ETO) qualification.

# Ship Types & Cargoes

Ships can be divided by ship size, engine size or type.

For deck officer qualifications, the STCW Code separates ships into vessels less than 3000 gross tons, less than 500 gross tons, or unlimited size.

For engineering qualifications, the STCW Code separates ships by engine size. Engineering certificates are restricted to engines less than 3000kW, less than 9000kW, or unlimited.

In normal life, it's more common to divide ships according to what they carry or what they do: passengers, cargo and offshore ships are the most common types.

In this section, I'll tell you a bit about what to expect on board different types of ships. Keep in mind that there are *always* exceptions and outliers, every ship is a bit different, and ships are constantly changing.

## Passenger Ships

*The cruise ship Carnival Victory*

When most people think of passenger ships, they think of the big cruise ships carrying thousands of passengers. These are definitely passenger ships, but they're not the only ones.

Any merchant ship that's allowed to carry twelve or more passengers is classed as a passenger ship. Ferries, hospital ships, sail training ships, commercial yachts, and even some research ships are also classed as passenger ships.

*Pros*

On average, the food and living conditions tend to be a bit better than most cargo ships, the cargo is slightly cleaner, and the crew tend to be more outgoing and sociable. The schedule is more predictable than on some other vessel types (passengers are less tolerant of being a few weeks late back from their holidays).

Passenger ships are often in port regularly, so there's more opportunity for shore leave.

Passenger ships are great for seafarers who like a predictable schedule, and who enjoy working with people.

## Cons

Someone once described passengers as the only self-loading, self-discharging dangerous cargo. It's cynical, but accurate.

If you work on a passenger ship you have to be ready to deal with large numbers of untrained customers in a dangerous environment while keeping a smile on your face and maintaining a pleasant demeanour.

## Cargo Ships

*A capesize bulk carrier ready to load at Whyalla anchorage*

This is by far the largest category of merchant ships. Cargo can be separated into dry cargo and liquid cargo. Most ships carry one or the other, although there are some exceptions.

Dry cargoes include containers, bulk cargoes (powders like

coal and grain), vehicles, heavy lift cargoes (oil rigs, other ships) and general cargoes (everything else from live animals to windmill blades).

Liquid cargoes are normally carried on specialised ships, and include oil, gas, bitumen, and chemicals. Cement is one of the exceptions: it's technically a solid, but because it acts like a liquid it's often carried on specialised cement tankers.

In general, tankers have a better safety record than dry cargo ships.

*Pros*

Cargo ships usually have the smallest number of crew that the company can get away with. That means you get to know everyone on board, adversity and shared discomfort can create a tight team, and everyone gets as much (or slightly more) responsibility as they can handle.

Cargo ships are great for people who are independent, like a challenge, and enjoy their own company.

*Cons*

Schedules on certain types of cargo ships are unpredictable. Large bulk carriers or tankers frequently get stuck at anchor for weeks or months, while some other types like container ships are a bit more predictable.

The only people on board are the crew, so the accommodation, food and facilities on some cargo ships can be pretty basic. The Maritime Labor Convention (MLC) sets minimum requirements. The requirements are quite low.

Because the crews are so small, it means that the work is

constant, there's often very little time to socialise or teach, and there's pressure to keep working if you're sick or injured.

## Offshore Ships

*Dive support vessel Bibby Polaris. Photo by Alan Jamieson.*

Offshore ships are ships that are associated with the offshore oil and gas industry. They include platform support and supply vessels, seismic survey vessels, pipe layers, rock dumpers, and many other specialised types.

Unlike cargo ships, offshore ships often have comparatively large crews for their size because of their specialised operations.

*Pros*

Usually short, predictable trip lengths, varied work, decent conditions, a good safety culture, and more opportunity to socialise outside working hours.

*Cons*

Working in the oil and gas industry might not suit people who feel strongly about protecting the environment.

## Other Ships

There are plenty of ship types that I haven't covered here, including fisheries protection, tugs, research vessels, yachts, dredgers, fishing boats, and many others.

Each of these types has its own pros and cons. With so many options, you're sure to find something that interests you.

## Operating Areas

Ships operate all over the world. Where your ship operates makes a big difference to your experience on board.

*Kapitan Dranitsyn moored in the ice near the French sailing vessel Tara. Photo by NOAA on Unsplash*

You can think about operating areas in three different ways:

1. Legal;
2. Insurance; and
3. Practical.

Standards of Training and Certification for Watchkeepers (STCW) is the international agreement that regulates the training of seafarers. Under STCW, there are two operating areas (near coastal; and unlimited) which require different training and qualifications.

Insurance divides ship areas according to risk: how likely is the ship to require an insurance payout in that area. A ship operating in areas of war, piracy, and high latitudes are higher risk than a ship operating in temperate latitudes.

What you're probably more interested in is interest, comfort and safety: the practical considerations.

If you're sailing through the Baltic in winter, you'll have a very different trip to your friend working in heavy fishing traffic in the East China Sea, avoiding cyclones in Northern Australia or standing pirate watches in West Africa.

## Coasters vs Deep-Sea Ships

As the name suggests, deep-sea ships are ships that operate far from land, while coasters work close to shore.

Coasters tend to be smaller ships on shorter trips with frequent port visits. The advantage of coasting is that you get to see a lot of ports and it's easy to leave the ship if you need to; the disadvantage is that the port stays are often short, and the work is constant.

Deep-sea ships tend to have longer voyages, spend longer in port, and are more relaxed between ports.

## Weather

Ships operating in high latitudes are more likely to encounter strong winds and ice.

Ships operating in the tropics are more likely to encounter tropical revolving storms (also known as cyclones, typhoons and hurricanes).

Some parts of the world have a lot of fog. This includes NW Europe, East China, and the Grand Banks in the North Atlantic.

# 4

# Frequently Asked Questions

**Why would I want to work on ships?**

Good wages, good leave, and not many expenses while on board, travel, freedom, balance of responsibility and interest, variety, and self-sufficiency are just some of the reasons seafarers give for working at sea.

**How can I get work on ships with no experience?**

It's difficult to get work on ships with no experience. There are charities and museums where you can volunteer to work on ships and gain experience that way, and cruise ships and yachts take a lot of staff who aren't from a seafaring background.

If you have cooking experience ashore, you may be able to complete your basic safety courses and find work as an assistant cook or steward.

## Are ships bad for the environment?

Cargo ships produce less carbon dioxide per ton-mile than other modes of cargo transport. Ships produce 0.0403 kg/TM, compared to air cargo (0.8063 kg/TM), trucks (0.1693 kg/TM) and trains (0.1048 kg/TM[2]).

## Can couples work on ships together?

It's unusual on most ships. The exceptions are on yachts and cruise ships.

## Do slaves work on ships?

Most ships are fair and reasonable workplaces. Unfortunately, modern slavery does occur on ships and it's mostly overlooked.

Ian Urbina's excellent book, "The Outlaw Ocean[3]," explores the subject in detail, and many organisations and governments, including the ITF, are working to combat slavery and human trafficking in the shipping industry[4].

# II

# Jobs in the Merchant Navy

5

# Departments and Ranks

There are three main departments on board every ship:

1. deck;
2. engineering; and
3. catering.

Within each department, crew are split into officers and ratings. The officers run things, ratings work under the direction of the officers.

The deck department is responsible for navigation, ship and cargo operations, maintenance of the hull and deck equipment, medical, safety, security and any odd jobs that pop up.

Deck officers and deck ratings, including able seafarers (ABs), ordinary seafarers (OSs), and integrated ratings (IRs) work in the deck department.

The engineering department keeps things working: the engines, generators, steering, pumps, electricity and hydraulics are all the responsibility of the engineering department.

Engineers, electro-technical officers (ETOs), and engineering ratings, including wipers, oilers, motormen, electro-technical ratings and integrated ratings (IRs) work in the engineering department.

The catering department has the important job of making sure we're all fed, and the communal areas are kept clean. If there's time, or if the weather is bad, the deck department often helps with the cleaning.

Cooks and stewards work in the catering department.

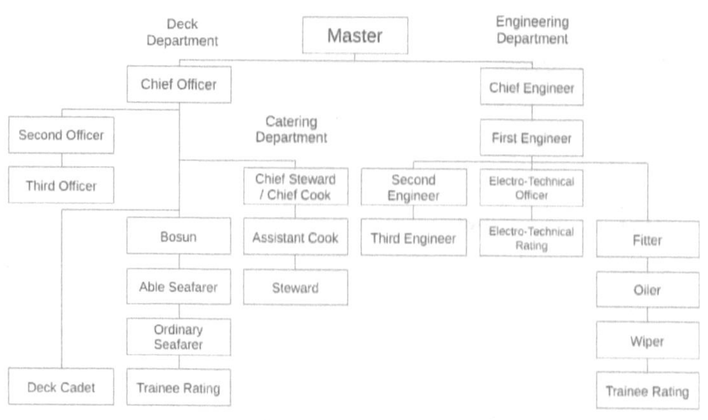


*The general hierarchy of a typical merchant ship*

While the hierarchy is more-or-less the same across the industry, the exact names of the ranks vary between countries and companies.

# 6

# Watch Systems

"Watch" is the maritime word for "shift". Most ships work 24/7, which means that someone always has to be up and working. There are several common watch systems, depending on how many people are available.

If you're on a watch, you're responsible for making sure you have enough sleep before your watch, and you are ready for watch on time. That means that you need to be awake, properly dressed, in the right place, and ready to work.

Being late for watch or unfit to work is irresponsible and can endanger your shipmates.

## What do you do on watch?

The name "watch" is accurate: you watch.

## Bridge Watches

On the bridge, you're responsible for the safety of the ship and everyone on board.  At sea, the officer of the watch (OOW) monitors:

- the position of the ship in relation to the planned track to make sure the ship stays on course and doesn't run aground;
- the position of other ships nearby, to avoid crashing into them;
- the equipment and alarms;
- any jobs going on on deck that could become a safety problem;
- the radio, in case any other ships need help;
- possible pirates and security threats;
- the weather and weather reports;
- keeps proper records; and
- calls the master if there's a problem that they can't deal with.

The lookout and the helmsman assist the OOW by steering and keeping a lookout.

## Port Watches

In port, the OOW is responsible for monitoring the cargo, ballast, security and safety of the ship, and calling the chief officer if there's a problem.

## Engine Room Watches

In the engine room, the engineering officer of the watch (EOOW) monitors:

- the condition of all engine room machinery, to ensure that any problems are noticed and dealt with promptly;
- the status of any maintenance and repair work that's going on in the engine room;
- the number of people in the engine room and where they're working;
- levels of fuel, water and oil tanks;
- amount of water in the bilges; and
- keeps proper records; and
- calls the first or chief engineer if there's a problem that they can't deal with.

# Two-Watch Systems

## 4-on, 4-off

This is almost never seen on cargo ships, but you may come across it on yachts or traditional sailing ships. It's exhausting because you can never sleep for more than three hours and forty-five minutes at a time.

The watch times are 00:00-04:00, 04:00-08:00, 08:00-12:00, 12:00-16:00, 16:00-18:00, 18:00-20:00, 20:00-24:00.

## Swedish Watches (4-4-4-6-6)

This is a compromise between 4-on, 4-off and 6-on, 6-off. The watches are six hours long at night, and four hours long during the day - or they can be the other way around. The advantage is that everyone gets one six-hour sleep a day; the disadvantage is that the watches rotate daily.

The watch times are 00:00-06:00, 06:00-10:00, 10:00-14:00, 14:00-18:00, 18:00-24:00.

## 6-on, 6-off

This is common on small ships which only carry the master and chief officer, but it's sometimes used on larger ships during cargo operations. In this case, the junior officers (second and third mates) stand the watches and the chief mate is on-call.

The watch times are 00:00-06:00), 06:00-12:00, 12:00-18:00, 18:00-24:00.

## 12-on, 12-off

This is common on some offshore vessels and dredgers, but unusual elsewhere.

The watch times are 00:00-12:00 (second mate), 12:00-24:00 (third mate).

## Three-Watch Systems

## 4-on, 8-off

This is the most common watch system in the industry, has the advantage of tradition, and allows people to get a bit of rest between watches. On this watch system, it's normal to do two to four hours of work outside your watches.

The watch times are 00:00-04:00 (second mate, second engineer), 04:00-08:00 (chief mate, first engineer), 08:00-12:00 (third mate or master, third engineer), 12:00-16:00 (second mate, second engineer), 16:00-20:00 (chief mate, first engineer), 20:00-24:00 (third mate or master, third engineer).

## 8-on, 16-off

This is common in port on some ships. It gives the crew a chance to either spend some time ashore or catch up on sleep.

The watch times are 00:00-08:00 (second mate), 08:00-16:00 (chief mate), 16:00-24:00 (third mate or master).

7

# Deck Department Roles

## Deck Officers

### Master / Captain

The master is in charge of everyone and everything at all times. They spend a lot of time on paperwork.

They "drive" the ship when arriving or leaving port, anchoring, picking up or dropping off pilots, or in awkward navigational situations. They're always on-call and the other officers will call them to the bridge if there's a problem.

If they stand watch, it's usually from 06:00-12:00 and 18:00-24:00 on a two-watch system, or 08:00-12:00 and 20:00-24:00 on a three watch system. If there are enough officers, the master doesn't stand a watch.

## Chief Officer / Chief Mate / First Mate

The chief mate is responsible for the day-to-day running of the ship, all running of the deck department, cargo and stability, and most record-keeping. They spend a lot of time on paperwork, and they take over from the master if the master is incapacitated or ashore. The chief mate is usually the ship security officer.

The chief mate stands watch from either 06:00-12:00 and 18:00-24:00 on a two-watch system with the second mate, or 00:00-06:00 and 12:00-18:00 on a two-watch system with the master. On a three-watch system, they stand watch from 04:00-08:00 and 16:00-20:00.

## Second Officer / Second Mate

The second mate is responsible for passage planning, maintenance of charts and bridge equipment. The second mate is usually either the safety officer or the medical officer, and sometimes the master's secretary.

Technically, the second mate is under the chief mate, but usually they report directly to the master for day-to-day business.

The second mate stands watch from either 00:00-06:00 and 12:00-18:00 on a two-watch system with either the chief or third mate. On a three-watch system, they stand watch from 00:00-04:00 and 12:00-16:00.

## Third Officer / Third Mate

The third mate is responsible for maintaining the life saving appliances (LSA) and fire fighting appliances (FFA). If the second mate is the safety officer, then the third mate is the medical officer, or vice versa. If the second mate isn't the master's secretary, then the third mate is.

Smaller ships don't have a third mate, in which case the second mate is responsible for the third mate's jobs.

The third mate stands watch from 06:00-12:00 and 18:00-24:00 on a two-watch system. On a three-watch system, they stand watch from 08:00-12:00 and 20:00-24:00.

## Navigational Watch Ratings

### Bosun or Chief Integrated Rating (CIR)

The bosun is the foreman of the deck crew. They report to the chief officer, and oversee all deck maintenance and operations. They're generally the most experienced of the deck crew, and a good person for trainees and cadets to learn from.

### Able Seafarer (AB) and Ordinary Seafarer (OS)

These are deck ratings. They carry out maintenance, cleaning, painting and greasing under the supervision of the bosun. They stand navigational watches as helmsmen and lookouts under the direction of the officer of the watch (OOW).

An AB has a lot of experience, an OS has less experience

## Integrated Rating (IR)

A few countries, most notably Australia and New Zealand, have Integrated Ratings instead of ABs and OSs.

IRs do the same jobs as other ratings, but they work both on deck and in the engine room rather than one or the other.

## Pump Man

Tankers carry pump men. They're equal to the bosun in rank, but they usually work under the chief mate.

They open and close valves and take ullages and soundings (measure how full a tank is) according to the chief mate's instructions.

## Deck Cadets

Deck cadets are in-training to become deck officers. Everyone outranks them. They usually report to the chief officer, unless the chief officer has delegated their training to someone else.

## Deck Trainees

Deck trainees are in-training to become a ratings. Everyone outranks them. They usually report to the bosun, unless the bosun has delegated their training to someone else.

# 8

# Engineering Department

The chief engineer is in charge of the department. The person below the chief engineer is either the first or second engineer, depending on the ship, and the rest of the engineers are numbered from there.

Engine rooms on ships are classed as either unmanned machinery spaces (UMS) or manned machinery spaces. On UMS ships, engineers are usually day workers and work from 08:00 to 17:00.

On UMS ships, after working hours the engine room is unmanned. One engineer is on duty to check the engine room at about 22:00 and 06:00, and answer any alarms. The duty engineer usually rotates daily so each engineer has a day on duty, then a few days off.

Apart from taking their turn as duty engineer, each engineer is responsible for looking after specific equipment. Every ship has a planned maintenance system (PMS) that tells the crew what maintenance and checks are due.

# Engineering Officers

## Chief Engineer

The chief engineer, often just called, "Chief," is the head of the engineering department.

They spend a lot of time on paperwork, but they're always in the engine room during standby (arrivals, departures, and when the ship is going through a restricted area like a canal) and during major maintenance work.

In emergencies, they're responsible for the engines and engine room.

## First Engineer (sometimes known as Second Engineer)

The first engineer is responsible for the day-to-day running of the engineering department. Their job is similar to the chief officer, except that they're responsible for the engineering department rather than the deck department.

They're responsible for management, safety, pollution prevention, making sure all of the maintenance is done, and ensuring that maintenance and pollution-prevention records are up-to-date.

If the ship isn't UMS, the first engineer's watch is usually 04:00-08:00 and 16:00-20:00.

## Second Engineer (sometimes known as Third Engineer)

The second engineer is usually in charge of boilers, fuel, auxiliary engines, incinerator, air compressors, condensate and feed systems, fuel and fuel oil purifiers, and often bunkering (taking fuel or oil for the engines).

If the ship isn't UMS, the second engineer's watch is usually 00:00-04:00 and 12:00-16:00.

## Third Engineer (sometimes known as Fourth Engineer)

The third engineer is usually responsible for operation, maintenance and record keeping for the purifier, compressor, sewage plant, incinerator, oily water separator, fresh water maker, and other machinery that isn't assigned to anyone else.

If the ship isn't UMS, the third engineer's watch is usually 08:00-12:00 and 20:00-24:00.

## Electro-Technical Officer

Electro-Technical Officers (ETOs) monitor and repair electrical and electronic systems and equipment. This role is quite new and is still evolving.

## Engine / ETO Cadets

They're in-training to become engineering officers or ETOs. Everyone outranks them. They usually report to the first engineer or ETO, unless the first engineer has delegated their training to someone else.

## Engineering Ratings

## Engine Room Rating

All the engine room ratings report to the first engineer.

## Electro-Technical Rating

The ETR monitors electronic and electrical equipment and troubleshoots electrical and electronic control and power systems. They report to the ETO and the first engineer.

## Fitter / Welder

The fitter is an expert in welding, grinding, turning and gas cutting. They often work on deck as well as in the engine room, and report to the first engineer or chief officer, as appropriate. They're equivalent to the bosun.

## Motorman

A motorman is a combined oiler/wiper.

## Oiler

The oiler helps the engineers with maintenance and painting. They report to the first engineer. They're equivalent to an AB.

## Wiper

The wiper does cleaning jobs in the engine room and helps engineers with maintenance and painting. They're equivalent to an OS.

## Engine Room Trainees

They're in-training to become engine room ratings. Everyone outranks them. They usually report to the fitter, unless the fitter has delegated their training to someone else.

# 9

# Catering Department

All humans need to eat: it's one of many things we have in common. Not all ships need cooks. Under the Maritime Labor Convention (MLC) only ships operating further than sixty miles from a safe haven, and ships operating with more than ten seafarers on board must carry a cook. On other ships, it's common for the crew to take turns in cooking, with varying results.

If you've never been on a ship with a food problem, it's easy to underestimate the importance of the catering department in maintaining crew morale. If there's any problem with the food, the negative atmosphere affects all aspects of ship operations.

## Chief Cook

The chief cook works in the catering department. They plan menus, cook meals, prepare orders for food stores, and keep their department clean.

Cooking on ships can be difficult and dangerous, both due to the movement of the ship, and the wide range food preferences of the different cultures and religions on board most ships.

## Assistant Cook

The assistant cook works with the chief cook to prepare and serve meals, and keep the galley, mess room and stores clean.

## Steward

The steward, assists the chief cook with food preparation and service, cleaning, organising stores, and planning menus.

On some ships, they serve meals to the officers and clean the officers' cabins, but this is becoming rare.

# III

# Training

# 10

# Qualification Routes

The qualification that allows you to sail as a deck, engineering or electro-technical officer is colloquially referred to as a "ticket."

To get your ticket, you need to pass written exams, get a certain amount of sea time, and in some countries pass an oral exam.

The information in this section is loosely based on the current UK guidance. Most countries are broadly similar with regard to the time frames and the type of training involved, but the details may vary. Check the exact requirements in your country before you dive in.

## International Agreements on Training

You'll remember from Chapter 2 (Maritime Law) that there are two Conventions that relate directly to training and qualifications:

1. Standards of Training and Certification for Watchkeepers

(STCW); and

2. Maritime Labor Convention (MLC).

The MLC specifies that the minimum age of seafarers is 16, that they must be medically fit, and properly trained. It lists special conditions to protect all seafarers under 18.

STCW details exactly which courses are required for which jobs, what has to be covered in the courses, and how long the certificates are valid.

In theory, STCW certificates are valid worldwide. The reality is that it's hit-and-miss as to which countries accept other countries' certificates.

## Basic Requirements

To obtain any Certificate of Competency, you must:

- Meet the minimum age requirements;
- Complete the minimum period of seagoing service and workshop skills;
- Meet the minimum vocational and academic standard, sometimes including written and oral examinations;
- Complete ancillary technical and safety training; and
- Meet medical and eyesight standards.

If you are considering a seagoing career, get your eyes checked before starting training. If you don't meet the minimum standards for vision and colour vision, you won't be able to go to sea.

Before you join your first ship, you'll need at least the

following certificates:

- A valid medical fitness certificate; and
- Basic safety training certificates (see Chapter 13: Courses & Short Courses)

## Training Schemes

If you want to go to sea, there are several possible routes. The exact routes that are available depend on your country. Broadly speaking, there are two types of training scheme:

1. Sandwich scheme; and
2. College first.

Sandwich schemes alternate periods at sea and periods at college until you have the appropriate experience and academic qualifications to sit for your ticket. The UK, Australia, and New Zealand use this system.

In college-first schemes, cadets complete the whole academic course, then go to sea and complete all of the sea time. The Netherlands uses this system.

Some countries only issue combined (deck and engineering officer) tickets, while most issue separate tickets for deck officers and engineers.

## How long does it take?

For cadets, it's usually three or four years from starting your studies to getting your Officer of the Watch (OOW) ticket.

For ratings, it's usually six months to a year for a Watch Rating

Certificate, then another eighteen months to two years for an AB Certificate.

## Hawse Pipes & Cabin Windows

Traditionally, there are two routes to becoming an officer:

1. Through the hawse pipe; and
2. Through the cabin window.

*Anchors securely stowed in the hawse pipes*

On a ship, the hawse pipe is where the anchor chain goes

out through the hull. Coming "through the hawse pipe" is equivalent to coming through the back door of a house when no-one's looking. Hawsepipers are those who started as ratings, then worked their way up to become officers.

Conversely, coming through the cabin window implies someone who knew from the beginning that they were going to be in charge. Rather than starting at the bottom, they skip most of the "dirty" work and come in as cadets, or apprentice officers.

There are advantages and disadvantages to both routes.

In general, hawsepipers know ships inside and out, and understand all the details and tricks, but they often find it difficult to step back and maintain an overview of the big picture.

Those who came "through the cabin window" are better at seeing the big picture, but often lack the detailed knowledge that comes from years of dirty work, and they sometimes miss the details.

This isn't true of everyone, and people from both routes make excellent officers.

## Cadetships & Traineeships

Cadetships and traineeships are basically apprenticeships. Cadetships are usually for officers, traineeships are usually for ratings. In either case, the sponsoring company pays for your training, exams, and sometimes food and accommodation at college.

In some countries, the company placement is arranged by the college; in others, you have to apply to the company yourself.

You'll sail on your sponsor's ships to get your sea time, and they'll provide training and support until you graduate. Some companies guarantee you a job when you graduate, but this is becoming rare.

## Choosing a Sponsor

There are three types of company that sponsor cadets:

1. shipping companies;
2. management companies; and
3. charities.

Shipping companies are great if you already know what type of ships you're interested in working on, and they're more likely to employ you on completion.

Management companies and charities can often put you on a range of different ships so you can get a broader base of experience, but they're less likely to be able to find you a job on completion.

# 11

# Deck & Engineering Ratings

## Watch Rating Certificate

According to the UK Maritime & Coastguard Agency (MCA), to be issued with a Watch Rating Certificate (Navigational or Engine Room) you have to meet the following requirements:

- be at least 17 years old;
- have completed at least 6 months approved sea service in the deck department or engineer room - or 2 months sea service if you've completed an approved college-based training programme;
- have completed STCW basic safety training;
- have been assessed as meeting the specified STCW requirements and performance standards; and
- hold a valid medical fitness certificate.

# Able Seafarer (AB) Deck or Engine Room

To qualify for an AB ticket, you have to meet the following requirements:

- be at least 18 years old;
- have completed at least 18 months sea service in the appropriate department (deck or engine room) while holding a Watch Rating certificate, or 12 months while if following an approved training program;
- have completed STCW basic safety training and Proficiency in Survival Craft and Rescue Boats (PSCRB);
- have been assessed as meeting the specified STCW requirements and performance standards (in the UK this is the Efficient Deck Hand (EDH) certificate); and
- hold a valid medical fitness certificate.

# Electro-Technical Rating (ETR)

This is a new and developing position, and not all countries issue certificates for this. Among the countries that do, the requirements vary a lot.

To qualify as an ETR, you'll need to meet the following requirements:

- be at least 18 years old;
- have completed approved sea service of at least 12 months. This can be reduced to 6 months if you're in an approved training programme, or as low as 3 months if you have other appropriate qualifications;
- have completed STCW basic safety training;

- have been assessed as meeting the specified STCW requirements and performance standards; and
- hold a valid medical fitness certificate.

# 12

# Deck & Engineering Officers

I f you want to become an officer, you can either become a cadet, or become a rating and work your way up.

## Deck Department

### Navigational Watch Rating to Deck Officer

If you're a rating or AB and you want to qualify as an Officer of the Watch (OOW), you have to meet the following requirements:

- Be at least 18 years of age;
- Since the age of 16, have obtained 36 months seagoing service, including 6 months engaged in bridge watchkeeping duties;
- Hold the applicable ancillary and safety course certificates;
- Successfully complete an approved education and training programme;
- Pass written examinations in navigation, stability and operations;

- Hold a valid medical fitness certificate; and
- Pass the appropriate oral examination.

## Deck Cadet to Deck Officer

If you're a cadet, you have to meet the same requirements as a rating to qualify as OOW, except for the sea time.

If you're following an approved cadet training program, you only need 12 months sea time rather than 36 months. As with ratings, this must include 6 months' engaged in bridge watchkeeping duties.

# Engineering Department

## Engine Room Watch Rating to Engineering OOW

If you're an Engine Room Watch Rating or Engine Room AB and you want to qualify as an Engineering Officer of the Watch (OOW), you have to meet the following requirements:

- Have completed 24 months' seagoing service on merchant ships of at least 350 kW;
- Hold an Engine Watch Rating Certificate;
- Hold a valid medical fitness certificate.
- Hold the applicable ancillary and safety course certificates;
- Successfully complete an approved education and training programme;
- Pass written examinations in Engineering Knowledge (General; and Motor and/or Steam, as appropriate);
- Hold a valid medical fitness certificate; and
- Pass the appropriate oral examination.

To get a ticket that's valid on both motor and steam ships, you'll need to complete both sections of the written exam, and an oral exam that covers both types.

If you only complete exams for one type, your ticket will be limited to that type of ship unless you meet extra requirements to obtain motor and/or steam ship endorsements.

## Engineering Cadet to Engineering Officer of the Watch

If you're a cadet, you will be following an approved training program. If you're a cadet, you have to meet the same requirements as a rating to qualify as OOW, except for the sea time.

Instead of 24 months sea time, you must have 12 months' combined seagoing service and workshop skills training on merchant ships of at least 750kW.

This must include a minimum of 6 months' seagoing service engaged in watchkeeping or Unmanned Machinery Space (UMS) duties and 3 months' workshop skills training while completing an approved training program.

The workshop skills training can be completed at sea, in an approved training program ashore, or a combination of both.

## Electro-Technical Officers (ETO)

### ETO Cadet to ETO

If you're a cadet, you will normally be following an approved training program. To qualify, you have to have met the following requirements since the age of 16:

- 12 months' combined seagoing service and workshop

skills training on merchant ships of at least 750kW. This must include a minimum of 6 months' seagoing service engaged in watchkeeping or Unmanned Machinery Space (UMS) duties and 3 months' workshop skills training while completing an approved training program.

- The workshop skills training can be completed at sea, in an approved training program ashore, or a combination of both.
- Successfully complete an approved education and training programme;
- Hold the applicable ancillary and safety course certificates;
- Complete an approved High Voltage (management level) course;
- Hold a valid medical fitness certificate; and
- Pass the appropriate oral examination.

## Electro-Technical Rating to Electro-Technical Officer

If you're an electro-technical rating without an appropriate academic qualification and you don't complete an approved cadet training course, you must complete:

- 36 months of combined seagoing service and approved workshop skills training;
- The relevant modules from the approved Electrical and Electronic Engineering training program;
- The applicable ancillary and safety course certificates;
- An approved High Voltage (management level) course;
- Hold a valid medical fitness certificate; and
- Pass the appropriate oral examination.

## People with Electrical or Electronic Engineering Qualifications

If you have one of the following qualifications or experience, you may be exempt from some parts of the training for an ETO:

- A degree, foundation degree, HND, HNC, or apprenticeship in Electrical Engineering or Electronic Engineering; or
- An STCW Engineering Certificate of Competency.

In this situation, your seagoing service will be decided on a case by case basis. The required seagoing service will be between 6 and 33 months, and may include a minimum period of workshop training.

# 13

# Cooks & Stewards

## Cook

To be eligible to be issued with a Ship's Cook Certificate, you have to meet the following requirements:

- be at least 18 years of age;
- have completed a minimum of one month sea going service in any capacity;
- have appropriate training or experience (either a specific course for ships' cooks, a level 2 cookery qualification, or 12 months working in a catering establishment ashore);
- have completed STCW basic safety training;
- have been assessed as competent in food safety, cultural and religious catering requirements, and dietary requirements of shift workers; and
- hold a valid medical fitness certificate.

## Assistant Cooks and Stewards

To work in any other role involving food preparation, including assistant cooks and stewards, you need to:

- hold an approved food hygiene certificate;
- have completed STCW basic safety and security awareness training; and
- hold a valid medical fitness certificate.

# 14

# Courses and Short Courses

Throughout your career at sea, you'll do hundreds of short courses ranging from practical survival, to simulators, to leadership. This is a summary of the main courses that you're likely to do before you even get to your first ship.

## STCW Basic Safety

This course consists of five separate courses, and usually takes a week:

1. Personal Safety and Social Responsibilities (PSSR)
2. Personal Survival Techniques (PST)
3. Elementary First Aid (EFA)
4. Fire Prevention and Fire Fighting (FPFF)
5. Security Awareness

*MV Cougar Ace. Photo by Peter Stinson.*

## PSSR

Teaches you how about life, culture safety and pollution-prevention on board.

## PST

Covers topics around sea survival, including how to put on survival suits and lifejackets, enter the water safely, swim with a lifejacket on, launch a liferaft, and get into a liferaft.

*EFA*

You can't call an ambulance at sea, so this covers basic first aid techniques.

*FPFF*

Covers how to extinguish fires, how to use breathing apparatus and fire extinguishers, and how to rescue casualties.

*Security Awareness*

This course covers the basic information you need to enhance maritime security awareness. You'll learn to recognise security threats and how to maintain ship security.

## Other Short Courses

*Designated Security Duties*

As the name suggests, this is for people who have designated security duties. You'll learn:

- why ship security is important, and the roles and responsibilities of the organisations and individuals involved;
- what constitutes a security risk, threat and vulnerability to the ship, its personnel, cargo and operations;
- the capabilities and limitations of security methods, equipment and systems;
- how to maintain the measures in a ship security plan and related requirements; and

- how to maintain effectiveness of security arrangements, procedures and equipment, at all three security levels.

*Proficiency in Survival Craft and Rescue Boats (other than fast rescue boats) (PSCRB)*

Most people do this course after six months at sea; some do it at the same time as their basic safety training.

It includes practical drills in launching and handling inflatable rescue boats, life boats and life rafts, and procedures for maximising survival after abandoning ship.

## Ship or Department-Specific Courses

*Basic Offshore Safety Induction and Emergency Training (BOSIET) - Offshore*

Covers a range of knowledge and skills relevant to travelling offshore by helicopter and working offshore.

*Minimum Industry Safety Training - Offshore*

Covers the key safety elements for working on offshore installations.

*Helicopter Underwater Escape Training (HUET) - Offshore*

How to escape from a sinking helicopter at sea.

*Emergency Breathing System (EBS) or Comparessed Air EBS (CA-EBS) - Offshore*

How to use breathing support systems while escaping from a sinking helicopter.

*Global Maritime Distress and Safety System (GMDSS) - Deck Cadets*

How to operate all on-board communication systems in distress, safety and routine situations.

*Tanker Familiarisation - Tankers*

This is required for everyone working on a tanker. It covers basic safety and understanding of key concepts for oil, gas and chemical tankers.

*Signals - UK only*

All candidates for a UK OOW (deck) have to pass an exam in identifying signal flags and flag groups, and sending and receiving morse code by light.

*High-Voltage - ETO & Some engineers*

Teaches you to manage high-voltage operations on a ship. This includes familiarisation, safety rules and procedures, knowledge of hazards, and documentation.

## Refresher Courses

Most certificates are valid for five years, then you need to do a refresher course for each certificate to keep it up-to-date. Offshore courses are valid for four years.

# IV

# Your First Ship

# 15

# Your First Ship

A common concern of cadets and trainees joining their first ship is, "But I don't know what I'm doing!"

That's the point. That's why you're a trainee, not the captain or the chief engineer. The first time you join a ship, all that's expected of you is that you:

1. ask questions if you don't understand;
2. always be on time;
3. work hard;
4. do as you're told (within reason);
5. speak up if you see something wrong; and
6. stay out of trouble.

The most important item on that list is number 1: ask questions if you don't understand.

I have never told a cadet or trainee off for admitting that they don't understand what they're supposed to do. Competent officers would rather explain it several times than have to fill out an accident form, or spend several hours repairing whatever you broke.

If you want to do more than the bare minimum, here are some ways to stand out (in good ways):

- report in the right place, on time, awake, appropriately dressed and cheerful (or at least not sour-faced and grumpy);
- look for ways to take responsibility for simple, routine jobs once you've learned the basics. On deck, you might offer to take over the daily tank soundings or reefer temperature checks; in the engine room, it might be pumping bilges;
- actively learn the jobs of the junior officers in your department. On deck, this would include checking the LSA and FFA; in the engine room, engine room rounds, operating the purifiers, sampling boiler water, fuel and lube oil;
- good housekeeping is a critical part of safety on board. Make sure you clean up after yourself, secure your work area properly if you have to walk away for any reason, and if you see something wrong, either fix it or report it;
- actively participate in drills. Learn your role, do it well, then start learning the roles of the junior officers in your department;
- even if you're a cadet, learn from the ratings. They usually know more about most of the practical jobs on board than the junior officers do, and it makes sense to take advantage of that experience. It also demonstrates respect and humility;
- find out what jobs are coming up the next day and research them. If you'll be loading cargo, read the procedure in the SMS; if you'll be overhauling a generator, read the manual. It makes you look good when you take responsibility for

your own learning; and

- make an effort to learn about other departments as well as your own. All cadets and trainees can learn a lot from spending a few days in each of the other departments on board - including catering!

# 16

# Before you join

## Questions to Ask

When you're find out you're off to join your first ship, there will be a lot of things going through your head. Despite that, you need to ask some practical questions so that you can be prepared:

- What type of ship are you joining? What cargoes? What operating area, and what countries and ports does the ship normally visit?
- Do they provide overalls and boots on board, and are they available in your size?
- Do you have to wear uniform on board? If so, is it every day, or just occasionally? Whites or khakis? Do they provide it, or do you have to take it with you? Do they have your size?
- Do they provide towels, bedsheets, soap and washing powder on board? Most companies do, but there are still a few that don't.

- Will you be sharing a cabin?
- How long will you be on board?
- Where are you joining, and do you need to apply for a visa?
- Do you need any extra vaccines before joining?
- Does the ship have internet access? What are the restrictions?
- What sort of electric plugs are on board? What voltage?
- Who do you contact if there's a problem with your flights en-route? Write the details down on paper and keep it on you - if your phone dies, it's not much help if the details are on your phone.
- What are the direct contact details for the ship and the agent?
- Do they reimburse your travel to and from the ship/airport? How do you claim it, and what records do you need to keep?
- How do you get from the airport to the ship? If you'll be picked up, where should you wait, and how will they identify themselves and identify you? If you have to make your own way to the ship, find out how.
- What are the contact details for DPA, HR & Training Director? Write them down on paper.

## What to Pack

You'll develop your own list after a few trips. This is just a starting point.

Bag

- Choose a bag you can carry easily, as you may need to carry it a long way across dirty ground, up the gangway, and up several flights of stairs. Bonus points if it folds up or folds flat so that you can stuff it out of the way once you've unpacked. Duffel bags or good-quality rucksacks with wheels work well;
- Get a proper TSA travel padlock, and lock your bag before travelling. Each padlock usually comes with 2 keys, so keep one key in your hand baggage and one in your wallet or in your pocket;
- Take several good-quality garbage bags and keep them rolled up in an outside pocket of your hand baggage. They weigh almost nothing, and if you have to leave your bag in the rain, put it down in a puddle, or stand in the rain, they can keep you and your bag dry.

Clothes

- Take enough clothes (including underwear) for a week;
- If you'll be mainly in warm areas, take one good set of warm clothes; if you'll be in colder areas, take two or three sets of warm clothes and at least three sets of good-quality thermal underwear. Several thin layers work much better than one thick layer in the cold, and they take less space in your luggage;
- Uniforms: take whatever your company told you to take. If you'll be wearing white shirts, make sure you have some white t-shirts to wear under the shirts;
- Socks - take several pairs of decent boot socks, and lots of

thin socks. If you wear thin socks under the thick socks, it helps to keep your feet dry, and it means you don't need to squash so many pairs of thick boot socks into your baggage. Take more socks than you think you'll need;

- Boots - if you're larger or smaller than average, take boots with you. Wear them on the plane, or they'll make your baggage heavy. Don't forget to take them off when you go through airport security; and
- Sun hat, woollen or fleece hat or balaclava, several bandannas.

## Electronics & Security

- International plug adaptor. The sort that works worldwide is more expensive, but it's a good investment;
- Chargers and cables for your electronic devices. Take a few spares;
- Waterproof, good-quality red LED head torch. If it's not rechargeable, take a set of spare batteries; if it is rechargeable, make sure you take the charger. Red lights don't ruin your night vision, so they're really helpful when working in the dark. If you'll be on a tanker, make sure it's intrinsically safe;
- USB battery pack. Make sure it's fully-charged before you leave home;
- As well as your normal phone, take an old phone which is network-unlocked. If you get a SIM card overseas, you can stick it in the old phone and you won't risk getting spyware/malware on your normal phone;
- SIM card adaptors;
- Subscription to a VPN on your smartphone;

- Movies and music on a portable hard drive;
- Earphones or headphones, and a spare pair of earphones. Don't take a portable speaker - it's extremely rude to do anything to wake up the people in the cabins around you;
- If you're an engineer, custom earplugs;
- Extension cable & power board;
- Battery-powered wedge alarm & spare batteries, in case you need to feel safe in your cabin;
- If you have or will have internet access via your phone, get a suction mount. When you're in range, you can stick your phone to the window (if you have a window) and get a better signal to use your phone as a WiFi hotspot.

## Toiletries

- Enough sanitary products and medication for three times as long as you're expecting to be on board, and copies of your prescriptions in your hand baggage. Depending on the country you're travelling to, some medications are illegal if you don't have prescriptions;
- One box of over-the-counter cold & flu tablets (non-drowsy);
- Soap (unless it's provided on board);
- Shampoo & conditioner;
- Hairbrush or comb;
- Toothbrush and two tubes of toothpaste;
- Hand cream;
- Sunscreen (SPF 50+); and
- Insect repellent & malaria tablets if appropriate for your operating area.

## Paperwork

- Passport;
- Maritime Certificates;
- Two sets of good photocopies of all your paperwork. Store one set in a separate bag from the originals, and leave the other set with someone you trust at home; and
- Hard copies of your flight details, contact details for the ship, contact details for the agent, and contact details for whoever you're supposed to contact if you have a problem while you're travelling.

## Random Stuff

- 2 pairs of inexpensive polarised sunglasses (one of them will get damaged at the worst possible time);
- Snacks, if you have room;
- A small sewing kit for basic clothing repairs (a few needles, thread, a few spare buttons, a few safety pins);
- Small things to help with your hobbies (pens and pencils for drawing, wool for crochet or knitting); and
- Take a photo of your bags before you travel. If they go missing, it's much easier to show the photo than to try to describe the bags.

## Notifications & Other Preparations

## Bank

Contact your bank and tell them you're going overseas. It sometimes stops them from blocking your bankcard or credit card the first time you try to withdraw money in a foreign country.

Store the bank's overseas contact number on your phone, because they'll probably block your card anyway.

## Car

If you have a car that won't be used while you're away:

- contact your insurance company and ask if you can reduce your cover while you're overseas. You might be able to save a bit of money, but don't forget to contact them again when you get home; and
- disconnect the battery before you leave.

## House or Flat

If you have your own home and it will be empty while you're away, make sure the water and as many electrical devices as possible are unplugged before you leave. If you have alarms and security cameras, leave them on.

Ask someone you trust to collect your mail and contact you if any urgent-looking mail arrives. It takes the pleasure out of returning home when you find a pile of threatening letters for missing jury service or not paying a bill.

# 17

# Life on Board

*Looking up the gangway. Photo by Sonse.*

When you arrive at the gangway, if you're lucky someone will meet you at the bottom and help you with your bags. It's rare, but it does happen. Normally, the duty rating or the duty officer will meet you at the top of the gangway, check your ID and sign you in. Make sure your ID isn't buried in the bottom of your bag. Someone will show you to your cabin, and tell you what to do next.

Over the next few hours, you can expect to meet the captain and the chief officer (or purser, depending on the ship), go through your paperwork, sign the crew agreement, and be shown around the ship.

Every ship has a familiarisation procedure. The shortest I've seen took fifteen minutes; the longest was thirty pages long and took a month to complete. Whatever the procedure is, before the end of your first day, make sure you know:

1. where your lifeboat and muster station are, and how to get there from your cabin;
2. what the different alarms mean, and what to do when you hear them;
3. where your lifejacket and immersion suit are. Check them to make sure they're actually there, they're in usable condition, and you know how to put them on;
4. where the mess room is, and what the mealtimes are;
5. any quirks of the toilet system;
6. if you're a cadet, find the SMS, SOLAS Training Manual, and the Ship's Library; and
7. make friends with the bosun, steward, cook, and the junior officers in your department. They're the people who can help or hinder you the most, so it pays to stay on their good sides.

## Communications

Some ships let the crew use the satellite phone or VOIP, but this depends on your company. If you have access to the phone, some ships have a free monthly allowance, some use a phonecard system where you buy a voucher for a certain amount of time.

If you're close to the coast, your mobile phone may actually work. Before you make or receive calls or use mobile data, make sure you check with your mobile provider: unless you're somewhere like Europe, most providers charge much higher rates to use your phone overseas.

To save money, make sure you have a SIM-unlocked phone and buy a local SIM card in port. The Mission to Seafarers often sells SIM cards; if you buy one from a random port worker, you may get ripped off.

An increasing number of ships have internet access for the crew. For these ships, sometimes it's free with a data cap, sometimes you have a voucher system. Regardless of the system, be aware that it's not private. Don't do or send anything on your ship's internet connection that you wouldn't want your employer - or your grandparents - to see.

## Clothing and Uniforms

This varies drastically between ships and companies. Always ask before you join the ship. When in doubt, take two white shirts, a pair of pants and a pair of black shoes, just in case.

Passenger ships are more likely to wear uniforms routinely than cargo ships, but some cargo ships want all officers, the helmsman and the lookout in uniform when entering and leaving port.

On ships that don't routinely wear uniforms, t-shirt and shorts, jeans, cargo pants and tracksuit pants are usually acceptable. Overalls are often provided on board, but in most cases they're not allowed in the accommodation or on the bridge.


## Bad weather

Storms are sometimes avoidable, and what they're like depends a lot on your ship, your area, and the direction you're travelling.

Light ships like a bulk carrier in ballast, or a container ship tend to bounce around a lot; heavy ships, like a loaded VLCC tend to slam into the seas; container ships can roll violently (parametric rolling).

Ships travelling with the wind behind them (running downwind) tend to have a gentler roll, but are harder to steer. If the weather's really bad, they're at risk of rolling over if they go off course.

Before going into bad weather, the officers will go through a checklist to make sure the ship's properly secured. Something they rarely check is individual cabins, so make sure yours is secured.

Sleeping in a storm can be difficult. If you wedge something under your mattress to tip it towards the bulkhead (wall), it can help to stop you from falling out. If you're not too big and you have a desk that's secured to a bulkhead, consider dropping your bedding in the little hole where the chair normally goes, and sleeping there. Turn the chair upside down and tie it to something.

Sleep is important, especially if the bad weather continues

for several days.

## Emergencies

You'll spend a lot of time learning exactly what to do in an emergency. Until you learn more about your exact role, the basic procedure when you hear an alarm is:

- grab your grab bag (lifejacket, survival suit, warm clothes) and go to your muster station;
- make sure you've been marked off as "Present" by whatever means your ships uses;
- take your lead from the experienced crew. If they're all putting their lifejacket and survival suit on, you do the same; and
- stand quietly and wait for instructions.

## Meals

On your first day, hang back a little and check where people sit. There are often unwritten rules about who "owns" which seats, and accidentally sitting in the captain or chief engineer's chair is a good way to get off to an awkward start.

On a practical note, don't fill your cup or bowl as much as you normally would. Ships roll, and liquids slop around and make a mess. You can go back for seconds if you want more.

As with everything on board, be on time: the catering department can't start cleaning up until everyone's finished eating. If the mess room is too small for everyone to eat at once, don't take too long with your meal or someone else might miss out.

Don't forget to thank the cook. It's demoralising for them if the crew only ever complain about the food.

## Laundry

If you find someone else's clothing in the washing machine or dryer, it's courteous to put it in the next stage rather than just dumping it in a pile. If it's in the washing machine, put it in the dryer. If it's in the dryer, fold it neatly and clean the lint out.

Before using the laundry, either read the instructions carefully, or ask someone to show you how to use the equipment. The usual mistakes are forgetting to remove the lint from the dryer (and potentially starting a fire), using the wrong amount of washing powder (and clogging up the machine), or shrinking your clothes by drying them at the wrong temperature.

## Money on Board

There are two main ways of dealing with money on board:

1. cash advances (subs/subsistence allowance); and
2. deductions from wages.

If you need money to go ashore or buy something from from someone on board, there's usually a system for cash advances, often known as "subs". In most cases, you request it from the appropriate officer and sign for it. The amount will be deducted from your wages. There's usually a limit to how much you're allowed to withdraw.

If you want to buy something from the ship's slop chest (shop), you can usually just sign for it and it will be deducted directly from your wages.

## Social Norms, Tips and Tricks

### Cultural Awareness

In different cultures, things like meeting people's eyes, pointing, pouring your own drink, using the "thumbs up" or "OK" gestures, holding hands, and showing the soles of your feet can be interpreted very differently from what you might be used to.

Watch how your shipmates respond to you, and if you notice someone looking uncomfortable when you do something, consider privately asking them why.

### Conversations

Listen attentively. Take cultural and religious differences into account before you open your mouth and take the lead from others until you get to know them better.

Learn a few words of the other languages on board. Basic greetings and courtesies, and maybe a joke or a curse, can help to break down barriers.

Remember: you're the newbie. You're entitled to respect as a human being, but they're the ones who know what they're talking about, and you need their help.

## Inter-Department Rivalry

The engineers think they're the most important department because, without them, there would be no water, lights, engines or flushing toilets. They put up with the deck department only because they have to.

The deck officers think they're the most important department because they drive the ship and keep things running smoothly. Also, the captain is from the deck department, and the captain's in charge of everything!

The ratings think they're the most important because they actually do the work, not like those officers who just sit around, stare out of the window and do paperwork all day.

The catering department knows they're the most important department: if you don't feed the crew, everything stops.

It's traditional to complain about the other departments, but the reality is that all departments are essential to the running of the ship. Take the rivalry in good humour, and don't push it too far.

## Socialise

People will be more willing to help you if you're willing to fit in, get your hands dirty, and get to know them. Rather than hiding in your cabin, if there's a chance, go and watch a movie or play cards with the crew.

If you have free time (rare, but it does happen), find someone who's doing a job you don't know how to do, and offer to help.

## Personality Clashes

It's completely okay not to like everyone, but you do have to be able to work with them. If there's a genuine problem, talk to them directly; if you still can't solve it, then ask someone more experienced for help.

## Punctuality

Never be late. It's unprofessional, and the person you're relieving is just as tired and fed-up as you are.

## Shore Leave

If you get the opportunity to go ashore, take it. Once you're qualified, it's difficult to get away, so make the most of it, and make sure you get back to the ship on time.

If you're in a country where you don't speak the language, ask someone to write down where the ship is in the local language, and keep the piece of paper with you. If you need to get back to the ship, you can show it to a taxi driver.

If you have a smartphone, downloading the local map in something like Google Maps, and the local language offline in Google Translate is really helpful.

Stay out of trouble while you're ashore. In particular, don't take photos of military installations or personnel - many countries react badly to that, and it's hard to get back in time for your watch if you're in a military prison.

## Pranks

Shipping is a traditional industry, and things change very, very slowly. Unfortunately for you, it's a long-standing tradition to play tricks on cadets and trainees to see if they actually have either common sense or a sense of humour. There's usually no malice in it, so keep your brain engaged and be willing to laugh at yourself. If something is unsafe, talk to your head-of-department.

## Tips

- If anyone gives you an electricity bill for your cabin, it's a joke;
- Electric navigation lights don't need to be filled with lamp oil, kerosene, or anything else. They do, however, occasionally need lamps replaced, lenses cleaned, contacts checked, and boxes painted;
- You do not have to pay for a seat in the lifeboat or liferaft;
- You do not have to buy - or hire - a lifejacket or survival/immersion suit;
- Left-handed rope, left-handed scissors and left-handed sounding tape *reels* do exist. Left-handed chipping hammers, paint brushes, paint rollers, knives, pens, calculators, chalk, sounding *rods*, measuring tapes and rags do not exist. If you're sent to find a left-handed anything, think carefully whether it makes sense;
- There's no such thing as striped paint. Or tartan paint. Or light black paint. Or glass hammers;
- You don't need to catch grinder sparks in a bucket;
- You don't need to fetch sparks for the grinder - the grinder

makes its own sparks;

- Steam doesn't come in buckets, and you can't take a steam sample - or an air sample - in a bucket;
- There are no spare bubbles for the spirit level, the compass, or the bubble sextant;
- Speaking of bubbles, if you're carrying a spirit level, compass or bubble sextant, nothing bad will happen if the bubble touches the sides, or the ends;
- Electric plugs don't need batteries;
- Don't hold a sack of anything over your head unless you need to pass it to someone above you. Especially if someone nearby has a knife and can cut the bag;
- Long stands, long weights and terminal weights are exactly what they sound like. If you're sent for any of those, go and relax in the mess room until they come looking for you;
- Check your hardhat, gloves and boots before putting them on. Depending on the ship, I've seen red food colouring, chalk, urine, feces, ice, dead animals and live insects hidden in hardhats, gloves and boots;
- If you actually manage to find a skyhook, patent it: you'll be a millionaire;
- Hydraulic oil or fluid exists; pneumatic oil or fluid doesn't;
- If you're dealing with electrics or electronics, find out what a capacitor looks like. They can zap you if you touch them without discharging them;
- Only ask for a spur lash if you want to go swimming; and
- Never, ever leave your phone where your shipmates can get at it. If you have to leave it somewhere, make sure it's locked.

Unfortunately, some of the jobs are actually real, no matter how crazy they sound.

- Counting tablets in the hospital. Some countries (looking at you, Russia and China) have been known to fine the ship if you declare the wrong number of tablets;
- Scrubbing dried seagull poop from the decks and hatches; and
- Inventories of just about anything.

# 18

# Training Programs

As I've said before, the most important thing is to ask questions. Lots of questions. As a trainee or cadet, you're not expected to know everything, but once you qualify, you're expected to know (or be able to work out) a whole lot more.

If you ask a basic question when you're a trainee, no-one will thing anything of it, but if you ask the same thing when you're an officer, you will almost certainly look like an idiot. (nb. If you do find yourself in that situation as an officer, ask anyway: it's better to look like an idiot for a moment than to screw up and kill someone).

## Training Record Books

If you're following a structured training program, you'll have a training record book. They vary, but you'll probably need to get some things signed off by the officers, and write some reports for college.

The most important thing is to take responsibility for your

own training.

Everyone on board has their own job and their own responsibilities. If you don't do any work on your book for six months, it's likely that no-one will notice. But they won't be happy if you turn up ten minutes before they leave the ship and ask them to sign six months worth of training tasks.

Stay on top of your training record book. Find out what you need to get signed off, and get someone to sign it as soon as possible after you complete the task.

Look through your book at the beginning of the trip, identify the tasks that might be difficult to complete, and ask for help with them.

Set aside some time once a week to work on your reports, and if you have nothing to do, go and learn something new. Visit a different department. If you're an engineer, visit the bridge; if you're on deck, visit the engine room; spend a day in the galley. Talk to people, offer to help, ask questions, and just be open to learning.

## Deck Cadets

The main things to focus on are:

- learn the colregs;
- practice filling in the log book, GMDSS log book and compass error book. If you're not allowed to write in them, make your own on scrap paper, and fill that in instead;
- don't be afraid to ask for changes to your watches or work assignments so that you can learn something different;
- offer to help with chart and publication corrections;
- shadow the junior officers - you'll have their jobs sooner

than you think; and

- ask for permission to stay in the engine room for a few arrivals and departures. It'll be your last chance to see what they're doing down there.

## Engineering and ETO Cadets

The main things to focus on are:

- practice filling in the engine room log book and oil record book. If you're not allowed to write in them, make your own on scrap paper, and fill that in instead;
- trace the pipelines and learn the positions and functions of all the valves;
- don't be afraid to ask for changes to your watches or work assignments so that you can learn something different;
- offer to help with routine jobs and checks;
- shadow the junior engineers - you'll have their jobs sooner than you think
- ask for permission to stay on the bridge and at mooring stations for a few arrivals and departures. It'll be your last chance to see what they're doing up there.

# 19

# Dealing with Problems

There are a lot of things that can go wrong at sea. You'll be trained in the practical stuff that affects everyone on board, things like firefighting and first aid. When you feel like you're the only one affected by something, it can be challenging to deal with.

## Seasickness

There are only three proven ways to deal with seasickness:

1. go ashore;
2. take medication; or
3. manage it.

Since going ashore isn't an option in most cases, here's some information about the other two.

## Medication

*Pros*

- Quick fix

*Cons*

- Drowsiness;
- You need to remember to take the tablets before getting seasick; and
- Because your body doesn't adjust, if you stop taking the tablets, you'll probably get seasick again.

*Tips*

- Don't forget to take the tablets;
- Make sure you have enough to last the whole trip;
- Make sure you know the correct dosage; and
- If they make you drowsy, don't take them at the beginning of your watch.

## Management

*Pros*

- It gives your body a chance to adjust naturally. It may last a few days on your first few trips, but over time it will be less of a problem; and
- You don't need to remember to take medicines.

*Cons*

- You'll get teased by your shipmates. Ignore them, it's just a tradition, and they'll respect you for working through it; and
- You'll spend a few days wishing you were dead.

*Tips*

- Stay hydrated and keep eating. Throwing up on an empty stomach is painful;
- Eat things that are soft on the way up, and not too acidic. Rice, toast, crackers and noodles are good choices;
- Eating ginger or drinking ginger tea can sometimes help;
- Stay where you can see the horizon;
- Stay close to midships - it moves less;
- If you need to throw up, make sure you're on the lee side with the wind at your back, otherwise it will blow back into your face;
- Sleep with a bucket, paper towels or rags, and a water bottle next to your bunk (secure them, or they'll roll away); and
- Remember, it *will* pass.

## Illness & Injury

Seafarers are notorious for not reporting illnesses and injuries on board. Don't do this, for several reasons:

- You're never off duty. If you're on an emergency team and your team leader doesn't know you're sick or injured, you could endanger someone else's life;

- If you have something contagious, you need to report it in case it spreads; and
- Insurance. If you don't report a minor injury that later gets worse, it might not be covered by the company's insurance policy.

If it's non-urgent, wait until the medical officer's normal working hours, then tell them about it. If it's urgent or life-threatening, inform the duty officer immediately.

If you have underlying medical conditions, consider telling the medical officer when you join the ship, just in case something goes wrong.

## Stress

This is a common problem at sea, and there are lots of specific resources that can help you manage it. Seafarers' Help Information Program has published a great free booklet about Managing Stress and Sleeping Well at Sea[5].

Some common methods for dealing with stress, anxiety and similar problems are:

- breathe deeply;
- if you can, contact friends or family for a chat;
- write in your journal;
- if you're on friendly terms with anyone on board, talk to them;
- hug (or punch) your pillow;
- exercise or yoga;
- watch a movie (bonus points if it's with other crew mem-

bers);
- focus on the things you can control;
- plan your options;
- help someone else;
- look for the silver lining in whatever's bothering you;
- read a book or listen to music (with headphones);
- eat healthy food;
- meditate or pray;
- practice your hobbies;
- listen to free mental wellbeing audio guides, or use a relaxation app (Headspace[6] and Tide[7] are popular); or
- Contact one of the support organisations listed in the back of this book.

Try them out and find out what works for you - we're all different - and don't be afraid to ask for help. Asking for help isn't a sign of weakness.

## Homesickness & Isolation

If you get homesick, you're normal. Seafarers don't usually talk about it because a shipboard environment is very traditional, and discussing human emotions is often discouraged.

Despite that, most seafarers get homesick from time to time. It's normally worst around holidays and celebrations, for example Christmas and Birthdays, or when something is going wrong at home and you can't do anything help.

## Bullying, Harassment & Assault

The exact definitions of bullying, harassment and assault will vary depending on the flag of your ship and the country you're in at the time. Regardless of where the ship is from, people shouldn't be harassing, bullying, threatening or attacking you.

On ships, it's impossible to escape, particularly if the bully outranks you. Every company should have a policy on how to handle bullying and harassment on board, so check that first and decide whether following the procedure in the policy will put you in danger.

Keep records with times and dates of occurrences: it can help to prove what's going on. If there's someone you trust on board, talk to them about it. Even if they can't help directly, they might be able to be a witness.

There's a list of support organisations at the back of this book. You can get help from any of those organisations, from your designated person ashore (DPA), from whichever company official is responsible for your training, or from your training institution.

## Fear & Anxiety

Seafarers often joke that the job is 90% boredom, 10% panic. It's not too far from the truth, but that overlooks the often continuous apprehension or anxiety that a lot of seafarers feel when there's nothing actively going wrong.

The ocean is unpredictable, and that's scary. Fear of storms, pirates, and capsize are common. Fear of doing something wrong, of letting people down is common. Fear of losing relationships at home, of being a different person when you get home are common.

There's nothing wrong with being scared, but you need to learn to deal with it, and that means understanding it.

## Immediate Fear

*The information in this section is paraphrased from Deep Survival: Who Lives, Who Dies and Why?*[8] *by Laurence Gonzales. I strongly recommend reading this book to understand the factors that influence survival in emergencies.*

At sea, immediate fear can be caused by an alarm, an explosion or an accident. There's an immediate jolt of panic, hopefully followed by a few seconds of thinking, then appropriate action.

During a fear reaction, the brain and body change to try to promote survival. Chemicals increase your heart rate and breathing, they dump sugar into your metabolic system, and shift the distribution of oxygen and nutrients so you have the strength to run or fight.

It affects your whole memory system. Under stress, you can probably only perform simple tasks. You might not remember the most basic things, and your brain functions change: you can see less, hear less, miss more cues from the environment, make mistakes, and focus narrowly on the thing that you consider most important. It may be the wrong thing.

Some ability may remain for your brain to:

1. recognise that there is an emotional response underway;
2. read reality and perceive circumstances correctly;
3. override or modulate the automatic reaction if it is an inappropriate one; and
4. select a correct course of action.

Some people are much better at it than others, and you can improve with practice.  Practice and drill your emergency procedures until they become second nature. If you don't have to think about what to do in an emergency, when your instincts take over, you're more likely to do the right thing.

## Apprehension & Anxiety

For most people, this is harder to deal with than immediate fear because you have time to think and overthink.  One of the more useful strategies is to pick apart your thinking, separate actual facts from stories, and work out a plan to deal with the most realistic worst-case scenario.

Talking to a trusted friend can help to ground your thoughts in reality: reality is almost always less scary than all of the other options.

# 20

# Going Home

It's great going home at the end of the trip: you've had a life-changing experience, and now you can't wait to see your friends and family again. You need to be aware of something called "Reverse Culture Shock."

You've changed, your perspectives have changed, your interests may have changed, you've almost certainly matured, but your friends and family don't know that yet. They'll treat you as if you're the same person you were when you left.

It might be hard to relate to people at first. People often want to hear about what you've been doing, but they probably won't understand it. It can feel like your words just slide past them, and their interest will often wane quickly when you try to explain.

Most people experience this in some form when they get home after a life-changing experience. Knowing about it in advance can help, but it won't prevent you from feeling a bit lost.

One tactic is to practice your answer to, "How was the trip?" Pick stories that are easy for landlubbers to relate to. If they keep asking for details, tell them what they want to know; when they've had enough, they'll stop asking. That avoids the trap of boring them with things that are meaningful to you, but meaningless to them.

Your friends and family like you, but they don't actually need you. Salter describes this dilemma well in his 2010 paper "Do Seafarers Suffer From Culture Shock or do They Adapt?"[9]:

> *"When the seafarer arrives home, they have moved from a situation where they are constantly taking decisions, taking responsibility, to a position of idleness and leisure. While their family are very pleased to see them, they are a disrupting influence on their schedule and their lives.*
>
> *In her book "Homeward Bound: A Spouse's Guide to Relocation" (Expatriate Press 2000), Robin Pascoe defines reverse culture shock this way:*
>
> *"(It) is simply the shock of being home. Feeling like a foreigner in a foreign land is expected; feeling a stranger in your own home is not." But the seafarer may well feel this way and by the time they do fit back into their own home, its time to leave again for that next trip."*

# V

# Reference

# 21

# Glossary

## Acronyms

- ACAS - Advisory, Conciliation and Arbitration Service
- AMSA - Australian Maritime Safety Authority
- BOSIET - Basic Offshore Safety Induction and Emergency Training
- CA-EBS - Compressed Air Emergency Breathing System
- EBS - Emergency Breathing System
- FOET - Further Offshore Emergency Training
- HUET - Helicoper Underwater Escape Training
- MARPOL - International Convention for the Prevention of Pollution from Ships
- SOLAS - International Convention on the Safety of Live at Sea
- IMO - International Maritime Organisation
- LSA - Life Saving Appliances
- FFA - Fire Fighting Appliances
- MCA - Maritime & Coastguard Agency

- MLC - Maritime Labour Convention
- MIST - Minimum Industry Safety Training
- OPITO - Offshore Petroleum Industry Training Organisation
- STCW - Standards of Training and Certification for Watchkeepers
- TSA - Transportation Security Administration
- UN - United Nations
- UMS - Unmanned Machinery Space

# Ship Terminology

## Parts of a Ship

- Aft - Towards the back of the ship
- Bow - Front of a ship
- Bridge - Where the deck officers drive the ship
- Bulkhead - Internal wall on a ship
- Cabin - Bedroom
- Deckhead - Internal ceiling on a ship
- Forward - Towards the front of the ship
- Galley - Kitchen
- Heads - Toilets
- Mess room - Dining room
- Port - Left-hand side of a ship when facing forward
- Starboard - Right-hand side of a ship when facing towards the front
- Stern - Back of a ship

# Other Terminology

- Bunkers/Bunkering - Bunkers are the fuel and oil a ship carries for their engines and generators; bunkering is the process of loading bunkers
- Equator - The circle around the earth, halfway between the north and south pole
- Latitude - The distance north or south of the equator
- Longitude - The distance east or west of Greenwich
- Subs - Subsistance Allowance (Cash Advance)
- Swing, hitch, trip - The period spent working on board a ship
- Tropics - The area between 23°26.2' N and 23°26.2' S

# 22

# Useful References

## International Organisations

- International Maritime Organisation (IMO) - http://www.imo.o
- International Transport Workers Federation (ITF) - https://www.itfglobal.org/
- International Association of Classification Societies (IACS) - http://www.iacs.org.uk/
- European Maritime Safety Agency - http://www.emsa.europa.eu/
- International Seafarers Welfare And Assistance Network (ISWAN) - http://www.seafarerswelfare.org/
- Maritime Piracy – Humanitarian Response Programme (MPHRP) - http://www.mphrp.org/
- International Labor Organisation (ILO) - http://ilo.org/
- Human Rights at Sea (HRAS) - https://www.humanrightsatsea.org/
- Seafarers' Rights International (SRI) - http://m.seafarersrights.org/

## Marine Authorities

The IMO maintains a list of contact details for Marine Authorities. The current list is at http://www.imo.org/en/OurWork/HumanElement/-Documents/rptPartyAddresses.pdf

## Charities, Support Organisations and Professional Bodies

- Apostleship of the Sea - https://www.apostleshipofthe-sea.org.uk/
- Cassiobury Court - http://www.cassioburycourt.com/
- Crewtoo - http://www.crewtoo.com/
- Mission to Seafarers - https://www.missiontoseafar-ers.org/
- Nautical Institute - https://www.nautinst.org/
- Safer Waves - https://saferwaves.org/
- Sailors Helpline - http://sailorshelpline.org/aboutus.htm
- Sailors' Society - https://www.sailors-society.org/
- Seafarer Help - https://seafarerhelp.org/
- Seafarers' Link - https://www.thesilverline.org.uk/seafarers-link-group-calls/
- The Sailors' Society - http://www.sailors-society.org/
- Watch Ashore - http://www.watchashore.org.uk/

# Notes

MARITIME LAW

1    IMO website - http://www.imo.org/

FREQUENTLY ASKED QUESTIONS

2    Potential to reduce the climate impact of aviation by flight level changes,
     Ulrich Schumann
         https://www.dlr.de/pa/en/Portaldata/33/Resources/dokumente/
     cocip/Schumann_etal_AIAA_2011_3376.pdf

3    The Outlaw Ocean, Ian Urbina - https://www.theoutlawocean.com/

4    ITF Human and Labour Rights https://www.itfglobal.org/en/sector/
     fisheries/human-and-labour-rights

DEALING WITH PROBLEMS

5    Seafarers' Help Information Program: Managing Stress and Sleeping
     Well at Sea. https://www.seafarerhelp.org/assets/downloads/Managing-
     Stress-and-Sleeping-Well-at-Sea.pdf

6    Headspace Meditation App https://www.headspace.com/headspace-
     meditation-app

7    Tide Meditation App https://play.google.com/store/apps/details?id=io.
     moreless.tide&hl=en_GB

8    Deep Survival: Who Lives, Who Dies, and Why., Gonzales, L., 2004, W.
     W. Norton

GOING HOME

9    Salter, Ivor. (2010). Do Seafaerers Suffer From Culture Shock or do
     They Adapt. - https://www.researchgate.net/publication/282291542_
     Do_Seafaerers_Suffer_From_Culture_Shock_or_do_They_Adapt/

# About the Author

Nic has been at sea since 1995. She started working on ferries and sailing ships in Australia while still at high school. In her path to her Master's ticket, she's sailed on container ships, dry bulk carriers, fisheries protection boats, ro-ro/ro-pax ferries, yachts and a hospital ship, and lived and studied in four countries.

**You can connect with me on:**

🌐 https://nicgardner.com

www.ingramcontent.com/pod-product-compliance
Lightning Source LLC
Chambersburg PA
CBHW031349060726
47590CB00007B/2698